The Official England Rugby

SUPERSTARS

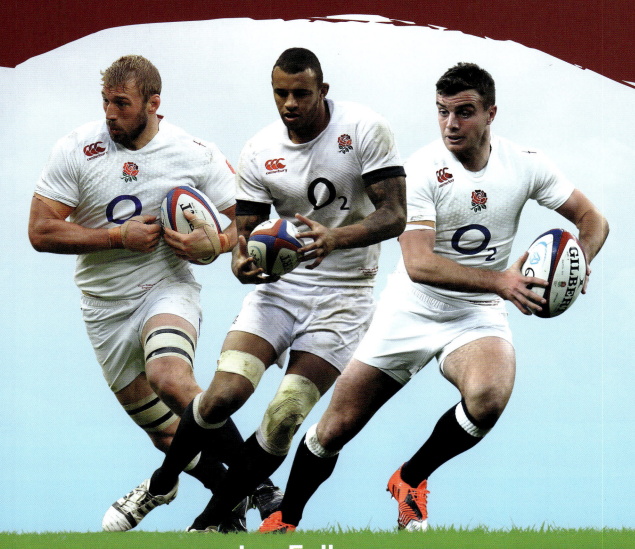

Joe Fullman

CARLTON KIDS

PLAYING THE GAME

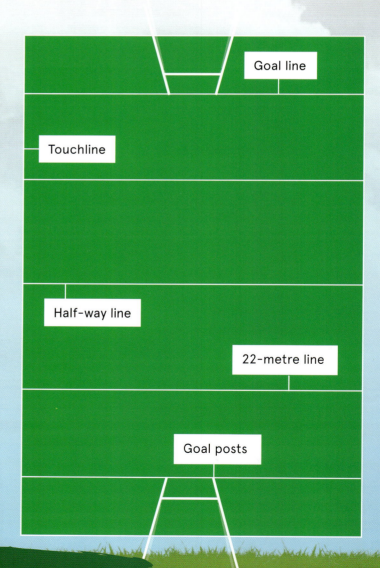

It's time to learn the basics of this action-packed game. Here are some of the important things you need to know.

TYPES OF RUGBY

There are different versions of rugby including 15-a-side, Tag, Touch, Sevens, Beach Rugby and kids' rugby. The rules are slightly different for each one. Kids' rugby isn't about big tackles, powerful scrums and fierce competition. It's about lots of tries, exciting action and working as a team. In your local rugby club you will play Kids First Rugby, which helps children get to grips with the game at their own pace and makes sure playing the game is fun. The 15-a-side game is what you will most often see on television for International, Premiership and Championship games.

It's important to know what the main lines are on a rugby pitch.

RUGBY WORLD CUP

The England team plays matches against other international teams. The most important matches take place during the Rugby World Cup, which is held every four years. For the England men's team their greatest moment came in 2003 when they won the trophy, beating Australia 21-19.

Victory! The England captain Martin Johnson celebrates winning the Rugby World Cup in 2003.

THE 15-A-SIDE GAME

Rugby is played on a large rectangular grass pitch. Two teams of 15 players – made up of 8 forwards and 7 backs – compete to score the most points using an oval-shaped ball. They can score by touching the ball down over the goal line or by kicking the ball over the cross bar between the H-shaped goal posts. A game has two halves of 40 minutes plus any stoppage time.

3

HOW TO PLAY

There are a number of activities in a game called set pieces. These include the scrum, lineout, ruck and maul.

THE BASICS

Kicking is used to start and restart the game, score points, gain territory or to defend the goal line by clearing away the ball. A team can also move towards the opposition's goal line by running forwards with the ball in hand. To pass the ball to a teammate a player passes it backwards. The opposition try to win the ball back by tackling the player holding the ball or catching the ball when it is passed between players.

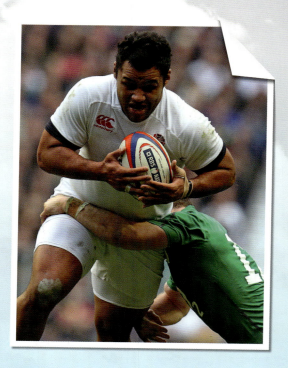

SCRUM

A scrum is used to restart the game when one team breaks the rules, by passing forwards for example. The forwards from both teams form a scrum, the team who was infringed against puts the ball in and both teams try to win the ball with their feet and move it backwards out of the scrum.

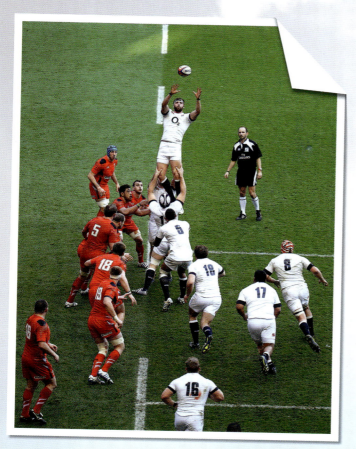

LINEOUT

If the ball is knocked or kicked over the touchline and into touch, a lineout is used to restart the game. The team that did not put the ball into touch gets to throw into the lineout. Players from both teams line up 1 metre apart. Then the hooker throws the ball down the centre of the space between the two lines of players, who attempt to catch the ball or knock it to a teammate.

RUCK AND MAUL

When moving the ball up the field to score, attackers will encounter defenders. In order to keep the ball moving forwards, the ball carrier can dodge past a defender, or pass backwards to a supporting player who is in space. However, if a defender stops the ball carrier, and they cannot pass to a teammate, then both teams compete for the ball in a ruck if they are on the ground; or a maul if they are on their feet. The team that wins gets possession of the ball and play continues.

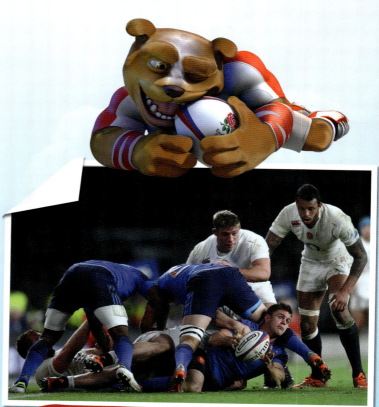

France perform a ruck to defend their ball as the England team attack.

5

MEET THE TEAM

DAN COLE

Born: 9 May, 1987
From: Leicester
Position: Forward – Prop
Height: 1.91m
Weight: 118kg
Current Team: Leicester Tigers

THE PLAYER

Dan was born in Leicester. As a boy, he was a big fan of rugby and grew up to play for his local club, the Leicester Tigers. He played his first game for them in 2007 at the age of 20. Just three years later, in 2010, he was picked to play for England.

THE POSITION

Dan is one of the biggest and strongest players in the England team. He needs to be strong to play in his position of prop. Props form part of the front row of the scrum where they push hard against the other team.

6

TOM YOUNGS

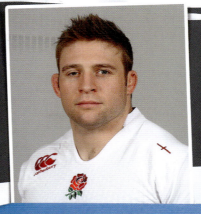

Born:	28 January, 1987
From:	Norwich
Position:	Forward – Hooker
Height:	1.75m
Weight:	102kg
Current Team:	Leicester Tigers

THE PLAYER

When Tom first played for England in 2012, he was welcomed by a familiar face, his younger brother, Ben. Ben has been playing for England since 2010. Both were following in the footsteps of their father, Nick, who played for England in the early 1980s.

THE POSITION

Tom plays as a hooker. During a scrum, the hooker's job is to try and 'hook' the ball with their feet back to their own team. Hookers also throw the ball back into play at a lineout.

7

COURTNEY LAWES

THE PLAYER
Born in London, Courtney grew up in Northampton and now plays for the town's rugby club, Northampton Saints. Since 2009, he has been picked more than 30 times by England. He took part in several matches during Rugby World Cup 2011.

Born:	23 February, 1989
From:	London
Position:	Forward – Lock or flanker
Height:	2.01m
Weight:	111kg
Current Team:	Northampton Saints

THE POSITION
Being 2 metres tall, Courtney certainly stands out on a rugby field. He can play in several positions, including flanker and lock. Locks play in the second row of the scrum and jumps up to try and catch the ball during a lineout. Courtney's height helps him to jump higher than many other players.

CHRIS ROBSHAW

Born: 4 June, 1986
From: Redhill, Surrey
Position: Forward – Flanker
Height: 1.88m
Weight: 110kg
Current Team: Harlequins

THE PLAYER

Chris is the current England captain. The captain is the leader of the team and its most important player. When he was younger, Chris played for both the England Schools Under 18 team and the England Under 21 team. He moved up to the senior England team in 2009 at the age of 22, and was made captain in 2012.

THE POSITION

Chris plays as a flanker. Flankers are usually very strong and do a lot of tackling. One of their main jobs is to stop players on the other team from running with the ball. They also take up the outside positions (or flanks) in the second row of a scrum.

BILLY VUNIPOLA

THE PLAYER
Billy was born in Australia but moved to the UK with his family when he was young. He grew up to be a skilful rugby player and was chosen to play for England in 2013, aged 20. His older brother, Mako, also plays for England.

Born: 3 November, 1992
From: Brisbane, Australia
Position: Forward – No. 8
Height: 1.88m
Weight: 126kg
Current Team: Saracens

THE POSITION
Billy is a No. 8. This position takes part in the scrum, pushing from the back. They are also often the first person to pick up the ball after a scrum. They can choose to run with it or pass it to the scrum half.

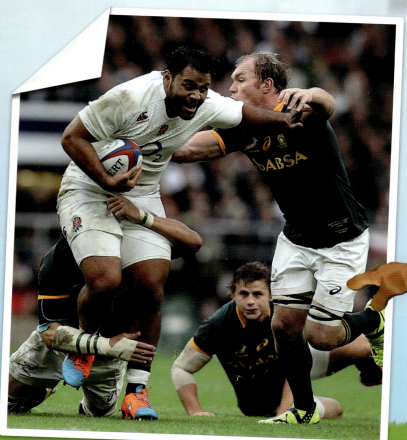

BEN YOUNGS

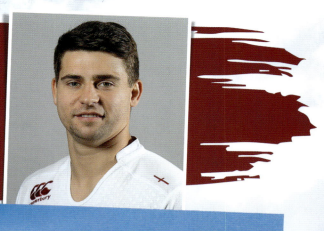

Born:	5 September, 1989
From:	Norwich
Position:	Back – Scrum Half
Height:	1.78m
Weight:	92kg
Current Team:	Leicester Tigers

THE PLAYER

Part of a rugby-playing family, Ben has had a very successful England career. He has played for the England Under 16s, Under 18s and Under 20s teams. In 2010, he played his first match for the senior England team.

THE POSITION

As a scrum half, Ben is the main link between the forwards and the backs. He feeds the ball into the scrum, and gets it passed to him from the back of the scrum and at lineouts. He then passes it to other backs, usually the fly half.

GEORGE FORD

THE PLAYER
George has been one of the country's top rugby players from a very young age. In 2009, he became the country's youngest ever professional player – in his first match for his club, Leicester Tigers, he was just 16 years and 237 days old. He played for England for the first time in 2014.

Born:	16 March, 1993
From:	Oldham
Position:	Back – Fly Half
Height:	1.75m
Weight:	84kg
Current Team:	Bath Rugby

THE POSITION
George is a fly half, the team's main decision maker. After a scrum, the fly half will usually be passed the ball and decide what to do next. He will either run with it, kick it or pass it to one of the other backs. A fly half has to be good at kicking.

12

MARLAND YARDE

THE PLAYER

Marland was 9 years old when he left the country he was born in, St Lucia. He travelled with his family to England where he began playing rugby at the age of 14. He quickly became very good and in 2013, at the age of 21, he was picked to play for England.

Born:	20 April, 1992
From:	St Lucia
Position:	Back – Winger
Height:	1.85m
Weight:	88kg
Current Team:	Harlequins

THE POSITION

Quick and agile, Marland plays as a winger. Two of the 15 players in a team are wingers. They play out wide on either side of the pitch. They need to be good at catching the ball and very fast so they can outrun other players. Wingers score many of the team's tries.

13

BRAD BARRITT

THE PLAYER
Though he now plays for England, Brad was born and grew up in South Africa. He even played for South Africa's Under 21 rugby team. However, because he had English relatives, he was allowed to switch countries. Since 2012 Brad has played more than 20 times for England.

Born: 7 August, 1986
From: Durban, South Africa
Position: Back – Centre
Height: 1.86m
Weight: 95kg
Current Team: Saracens

THE POSITION
Brad plays as one of two centres in the rugby team. They mainly play between the fly half and one of the wingers. They do a lot of passing, helping to get the ball from the scrum to the wingers. They also make a lot of tackles and score lots of tries.

MIKE BROWN

THE PLAYER
Since 2007, Mike has played more than 30 times for England. He is a quick player and a very good catcher and kicker of the ball. He has scored quite a few tries for his country.

Born: 4 September, 1985
From: Southampton
Position: Back – Full Back
Height: 1.83m
Weight: 89kg
Current Team: Harlequins

THE POSITION
Mike plays full back. Full backs are positioned at the back of the rugby team. Their role includes kicking balls downfield, passing, and catching balls kicked forward by the other team. As the last man, it's often their job to stop the other team from scoring tries.

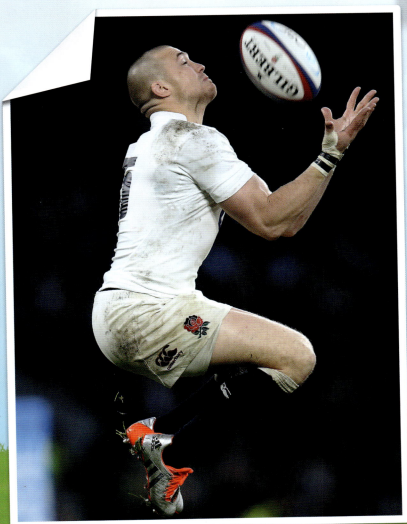

ENGLAND WOMEN

The first mention of women playing rugby was as early as the late 1800s, however it was not until the late 19th century that women started playing in greater numbers and in 1982, the England Women's rugby team was formed. Today Women's rugby is one of the fastest growing team sports in the UK.

TWO-TIME WORLD CHAMPIONS

Just like the men, the England Women's rugby team takes part in several important competitions. These include the Six Nations Championship, held every year, and the Rugby World Cup, held every four years. England has won the Rugby World Cup twice. In 1994, they defeated the USA 38–33, and in 2014 they beat Canada 21–9. They have also won the Six Nations seven years in a row, from 2006-2012.

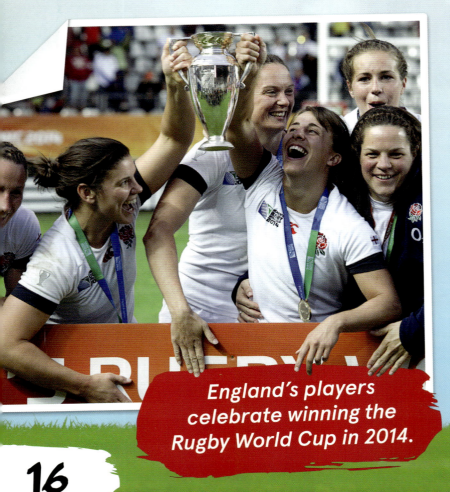

England's players celebrate winning the Rugby World Cup in 2014.

KATY MCLEAN   EMILY SCARRATT

THE PLAYER
Katy, who plays fly half, was in the England team that lost to New Zealand in the Rugby World Cup 2010 final. Afterwards she became captain, and in 2014 she led the team to victory over Canada. For many years, Katy also worked as a primary school teacher. However, she is now a full time rugby player after being offered a professional contract in 2014.

THE PLAYER
Emily played lots of different sports when she was young, including basketball and hockey. But rugby was the one she liked best. She grew up to become one of England Women's best players. At Rugby World Cup 2014, she was the tournament's top scorer with 70 points.

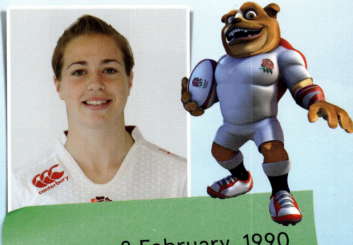

Born: 19 December, 1985
From: South Shields
Position: Fly Half
Height: 1.67m
Weight: 70kg
Current Team: Darlington Mowden Park Sharks

Born: 8 February, 1990
From: Leicester
Position: Centre – Full Back
Height: 1.81m
Weight: 78kg
Current Team: Lichfield

ENGLAND U20

The players in the main men's England rugby team are usually in their twenties and thirties. However, younger players can also play for their country as a member of the England Under 20s side. To be picked, players have to be aged 20 or under on January 1 of the year they play. They also have to be very good at rugby, of course!

WORLD CHAMPIONS

The U20 team competes in the World Rugby Under 20 Championship, which has been held every year since 2008. England were runners up three times, in 2008, 2009 and 2011. However, they upped their game and finally won the trophy by beating Wales in 2013. The next year, they defended their crown by defeating South Africa.

DID YOU KNOW? The youngest player to be picked for the main England side was Colin Laird. He was just 18 years and 134 days old when he played for England against Wales in 1927.

England's junior players enjoy their victory in the 2013 Word Rugby Under 20 Championship.

ENGLAND 7S

Sevens is a quick, high-scoring version of rugby that was invented in Scotland in the late 19th century. It's played on the same size pitch as the standard game. However, there are just seven players on each team, rather than 15.

RUGBY WORLD CUP SEVENS

Just like the 15-man version of the game, there is a Rugby World Cup tournament for the sevens teams. It began in 1993 and has been held every four years since. England won the first tournament and came second in the last one in 2013, where they were beaten by New Zealand. Sevens is one of three new sports that will be introduced at the 2016 Olympic Games in Rio de Janeiro.

TOM MITCHELL

THE PLAYER

Tom is not just the captain of the England Sevens, he's also one the team's best players and highest scorers. Since he first played for the team in 2012, he has scored more than 50 tries and racked up over 500 points.

Born:	22 July, 1989
From:	Cuckfield
Position:	Fly Half – Centre
Height:	1.77m
Weight:	86kg

19

SPOT THE DIFFERENCE

These two pictures look similar, but there are actually eight small differences between them. Can you spot them all?

SPOT THE BALL

The ball has been thrown in for a lineout. Circle the square you think the missing rugby ball is in.

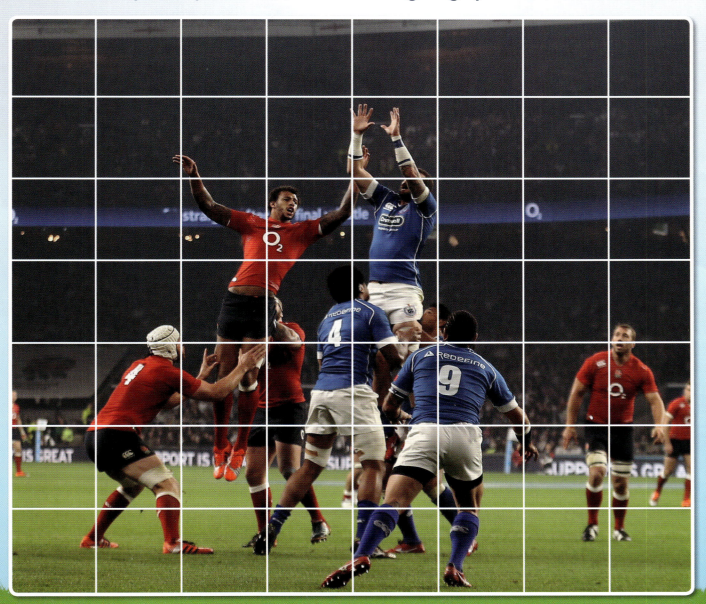

ANSWERS on page 32

21

RUGBY SKILLS

On the next few pages we'll look at some of the skills you need to learn to play rugby at your age. Master these and you'll soon be a top player!

PASSING

Passing is one of the main ways of moving the ball in a game of rugby. Players pass the ball to each other to move it down the pitch, and to stop the other team from getting hold of it. Remember, in rugby, you can pass the ball only sideways or backwards – never forwards.

DID YOU KNOW?
Rugby balls are oval shaped, rather than round, because the first balls were made of an inflated pig's bladder, wrapped in leather. As pigs' bladders are oval, so were the balls. These early balls also varied in size, depending on how big the bladder was.

22

How to pass a rugby ball

STEP 1
Hold the ball out in front of you, gripping it with your fingers spread.

STEP 2
Looking at the receiver who you are passing to, push the ball across your body towards them.

STEP 3
Aim to throw the ball at the receiver's hands, which should be in front of their chest to make it easier for them to catch. Release the ball in a backwards direction towards the player catching.

Find your local rugby club at:
http://www.englandrugby.com/my-rugby/players/club-finder/

RUGBY SKILLS

CATCHING

Rugby balls are oval-shaped, which makes them tricky to catch. It takes a lot of practice to become a good catcher. Dropping the ball during a game can stop your team from scoring or give the ball away to the opposition so they can score.

How to catch a ball at chest height

STEP 1
Stand about 5m to the side of the player who is throwing the ball and slightly behind them. Hold your hands out at chest height, with your thumbs up and your fingers spread out.

STEP 2
When the thrower lets go of the ball, keep your eyes on it until it reaches you. Grab it with both hands and bring it into your body.

How to catch a high ball

STEP 1
When the ball is in the air, move beneath it and stand with your feet apart. Put your arms out in front of your chest with your elbows close together and your hands turned inwards to form a cradle for the ball.

STEP 2
As the ball drops, keep your eyes on it until it reaches you, then catch it with both hands and bring it into your body – this will help to stop you dropping it, and protect it from other players.

DID YOU KNOW?
Today a try is worth five points. But when rugby first began, it wasn't worth any points. Instead, it gave the team that scored it the chance to 'try' and score a conversion by kicking the ball over the cross bar between the goal posts.

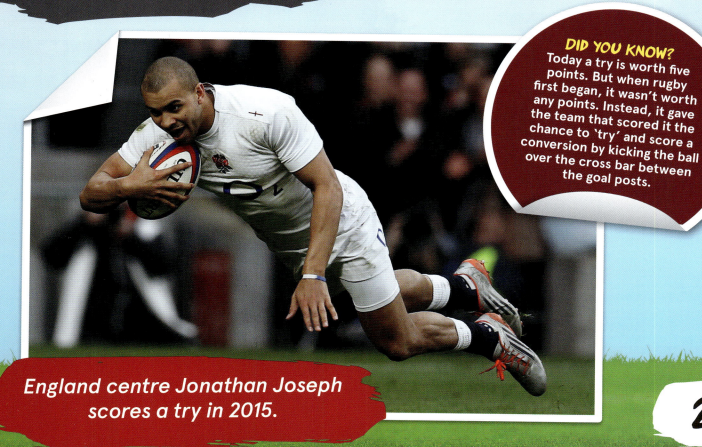

England centre Jonathan Joseph scores a try in 2015.

RUGBY SKILLS

TACKLING

Tackling means to grab hold of a player and bring them to the ground. It's the main way one team stops the other team from scoring, and it's a big part of the game. It's important that you tackle in the correct way, so you don't injure yourself – or your opponent.

How to tackle

STEP 1
You should approach the player you want to tackle from the front or the side. As you move towards them, keeping your eyes on the target and head up, push your shoulder into their thigh and wrap your arms around their legs.

STEP 2
Make sure that your head goes to the side or behind the other player – this will help to avoid injuries. Keep pushing into the other player using your legs and body weight until they start to fall.

STEP 3
With your arms still around their legs, use your weight to bring the player to the ground.

DID YOU KNOW?
This book focuses on rugby union, but there is another type of rugby, rugby league, which has slightly different rules. In the late 19th century, the clubs that thought they should be paid started their own form of the game – and rugby league was born. Today, both rugby union and rugby league players are paid.

England player Luther Burrell is tackled while playing Ireland in RBS 6 Nations 2014.

27

RUGBY SKILLS
KICKING

There are three ways to score by kicking in a game of rugby:

CONVERSION: After a try has been scored (five points), a player from the scoring side has the chance to score two more points by kicking the ball over the cross bar betweem the goal posts.

DROP GOAL: Drop goals are scored in open play and are worth three points. To score one, the player must drop the ball on the ground and then immediately as it comes back up kick it over the cross bar between the goal posts.

PENALTY KICK: When a team has had an offence committed against them, the referee awards a penalty. If the team are in kicking range of the goal posts they can choose to go for a penalty kick worth three points. The kicker places the ball on a kicking tee and then attempts to kick the ball over the cross bar and between the goal posts to score the points.

DID YOU KNOW? The longest ever kick in a rugby union game was made by an English schoolboy. In 1944 Ernie Cooper, a 17-year-old member of Bridlington School, scored a monster 74-metre penalty.

How to take a goal kick

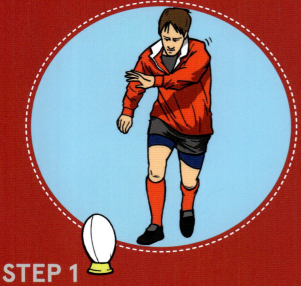

STEP 1
Place the ball on a plastic kicking tee or small mound of earth so that it is pointing towards the goalposts. To begin with, try kicking it from around 10 metres from the posts. You can increase the distance as you get better. Take a few steps back.

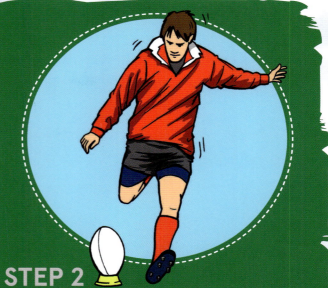

STEP 2
Step towards the ball. Place your non-kicking foot 10–20cm to the side of the ball and just behind it. Keep your head down and your eyes focused on the ball.

STEP 3
Kick the ball about a third of the way from the bottom using your instep – the curved part of your foot between your toes and your ankle. Make sure your leg follows through for maximum power and height.

Find your local rugby club at:
http://www.englandrugby.com/my-rugby/players/club-finder/

GUESS WHO

Can you tell who these famous England faces are? Write their names in the boxes below.

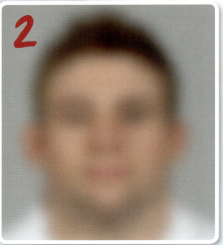

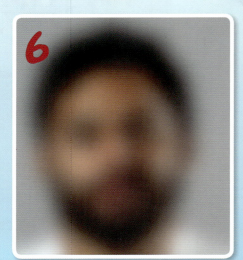

ANSWERS on page 32

JOIN THE DOTS

Join the dots to make a picture of Ruckley, the rugby-mad bulldog who's England's biggest fan. Ruckley loves playing rugby with his friends – and watching England, of course!

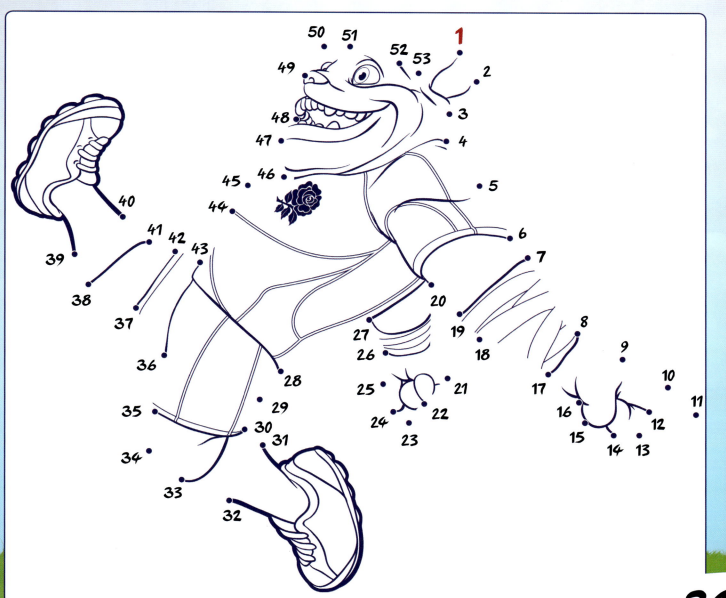

31

ANSWERS

PAGE 20 - SPOT THE DIFFERENCE

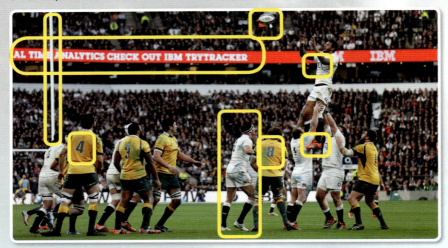

PAGE 21 - SPOT THE BALL

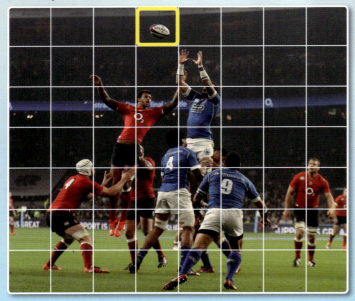

PAGE 30 - GUESS WHO

1. Tom Mitchell
2. Tom Youngs
3. Emily Scarratt
4. Marland Yarde
5. Chris Robshaw
6. Billy Vunipola

THIS IS A CARLTON BOOK
© Carlton Books Limited 2015

Editor: Tasha Percy
Designers: Darren Jordan & Rebecca Wildman
Illustrator: Andy Everitt-Stewart
Production: Marion Storz

Published in 2015 by Carlton Books Ltd
An imprint of the Carlton Publishing Group
20 Mortimer Street, London W1T 3JW

Rugby Football Union. The Red Rose and the words 'England Rugby' are official registered trade marks of the Rugby Football Union and are subject to extensive trademark registration worldwide.

RFU Official Licensed Product: The RFU guarantees that all profits from the sale of products and services carrying the Invest in Rugby Mark will be invested in to rugby at all levels in England. englandruby.com/invest

1 3 5 7 9 10 8 6 4 2

All rights reserved. This book is sold subject to the condition that it may not be reproduced, stored in a retrieval system or transmitted in any form or by any means, electronic, mechanical, photocopying, recording or otherwise, without the publisher's prior consent.

A catalogue record for this book is available from the British Library.

ISBN: 978-1-78312-143-4

Printed in China

Picture Credits
The publishers would like to thank the following sources for their kind permission to reproduce the pictures in this book:
Alamy: /Image Source: 22
Getty Images: /David Cannon: 5B; /Alain Jocard/AFP: 16; /Glyn Kirk/AFP: 1L; /Mark Kolbe: 5T; /MyLoupe/UIG: 2; /Adam Pretty: 3; /David Rogers: 6B
The RFU Collection via Getty Images: 17L, 17R, 30TR; /Steve Bardens: 20; /Tom Dulat: 18; /Tony Marshall: 19B; /David Rogers: 1C, 1R, 4, 7B, 8T, 8B, 9T, 9B, 10T, 10B, 11T, 12T, 12B, 13T, 13B, 14T, 14B, 15T, 15B, 21, 25, 27, 30BL, 30BC, 30BR; /Clive Rose: 11B; /Tom Shaw: 6T, 7T, 19T, 30TL, 30TC

Every effort has been made to acknowledge correctly and contact the source and/or copyright holder of each picture and Carlton Books Limited apologises for any unintentional errors or omissions that will be corrected in future editions of this book.